How Do You Find the Time?

A Guide to Time Management and Personal
Development Techniques That Can Double
Efficiency and Lead to Professional Growth

From the author of *Waiting on Zapote Street*

Betty Viamontes

How Do You Find the Time?

Published in the United States by Zapote Street Books, LLC, Tampa, Florida

ISBN: 978-0-986423789

Book cover photo by Betty Viamontes

Printed in the United States of America

Contents

To my mother, for showing me that anything is possible and for believing in the promise of America. For being a mother, a father, a friend, love, and benevolence. I miss you immensely.

To my husband, for sharing my life for over forty years and giving me the most amazing son a mother could ever have. We were two eighteen-year-olds with a baby on the way. The odds were against us, and no one thought we would make it, but the love we had for each other survived it all. Thank you for allowing me to be a daughter to your parents, the most unselfish people I know.

To my readers, for reading my books and encouraging me to keep writing.

Part I

Time Management

Time

Whether you live in a large metropolis, like New York City, Miami, or Chicago, or a smaller city, like Tampa or Jacksonville, Florida, we often hear working adults complain there is not enough time during the day to accomplish every task in twenty hours.

You might be stuck in traffic for over an hour on your way to work, or your subway train is delayed, or you have to stay in the office until late at night to finish an assignment. Something or someone always absorbs your time.

Parents, children, bosses, or a significant other: everyone demands more of your time. Time you don't have! Maybe you can sleep fewer hours. That may work. Train your body to function with less sleep. But you have read that sleep is important for critical thinking. You take a deep breath.

Time.

We never have enough of it. And everyone around you keeps competing for *your* time. You keep saying **yes** because you do not want to upset your boss or get into an argument with your significant other. God knows you don't want to hurt your parents!

If you have children, they want to spend quality time with their mom or dad. It is only natural. But how do you handle all of these competing priorities?

Time management.

Can you truly "manage" time? Is it possible?

How Do You Find the Time?

You keep hearing that term, and you are certain that people who write about time management have way too much *time* on their hands, *time* <u>you don't have</u>. Otherwise, they *would not* have the time to write or think about anything because they'd be too consumed with life!

You have heard the phrase: time is money. But time is more than money. It has an intangible quality to it.

How many of us yearn for those quiet moments of solitude when we can do what we wish with *our time?*

This book examines techniques that will allow you to manage this invaluable asset. It also explores personal development as an integral part of time management because the more we develop as individuals, the more confident we will be to take positions we've never dared to take before. We will learn when and how to say no, how to imply "no" without saying it, and how to ask the appropriate questions that will buy us more time.

The online Merriam-Webster dictionary had, as of the day I began to write this book, fourteen different definitions of time. The online Oxford dictionary has one all-encompassing definition: "The indefinite continued progress of existence and events in the past, present, and future regarded as a whole."

How do *you* define time?

Since the beginning of civilization, man has felt the need to measure time, which led to the invention of the clock. No one really knows when the first clock was invented. We know that it has suffered significant transformations, from sundials, the first time measuring mechanism known to man —created in Babylon over six thousand years ago— to mechanical and digital clocks.

Have you counted how many clocks you have in your house?

How Do You Find the Time?

As I sit on my sofa writing this book, I look around and see four of them: two digital and two mechanical. **Four clocks**. I have three more in our bedroom, one on each nightstand and the radio below the television set.

Could you go through your day without looking at a clock?

Chances are your answer will be no. This book will help you make the most of your time. It will help you improve efficiency in the workplace and allow you to apply some of these techniques, whenever feasible and practical, to your everyday life. It will explore how personal development can lead to professional growth and, ultimately, to efficiency.

This book is intended for managers and non-managers. In it, I'll draw from personal experiences because it's these experiences that have allowed me to conquer time finally.

My background, my over thirty years of management experience dealing with all levels of leaders, the numerous lectures I've attended, and even those I've taught allowed me to understand organizations and human behavior and to develop techniques that more than double efficiency in departments I've managed.

Over the last two years, I have:

- Written two books

- Translated three of my books into Spanish

- Worked as the accounting administrator (controller) for a large healthcare system, where I managed the finances of multiple entities with combined revenues of $1 billion

- Chaired the Florida Institute of Certified Public Accountants Healthcare Conference

- Managed my two residential rental businesses and a book-publishing business

- Spoken at local universities and professional conferences

- Served on the Board of Trustees of Hillsborough Community College and traveled to Tallahassee and Washington DC to advocate on behalf of community college students

As someone who started as an immigrant at age fifteen, not knowing English, people ask me: *How did you do it?*

I hope to share these experiences with you and, in the process, help you improve your work life, which will inevitably lead to a better life at home.

This book is organized into two parts. In the next three chapters of Part I examine situations that led me to do more with less at the companies where I've worked and to more than double efficiency.

The remaining chapters in Part I focus on the elements of time management and practical applications that will help you save time and have the potential to double efficiency.

Finally, section II discusses how personal growth can lead to professional development and a balanced life.

As you read each section, ask yourself:

How can I apply these concepts and examples to my personal circumstances?

People who attended my lectures have reached out to me, sometimes months later, and shared how they felt inspired and driven to do the things they always wanted to do but for which they did not believe they had the time.

But somehow, they found it!

Remember, the capability to achieve great things is within all of us. This book will help you uncover it.

I hope *How Do You Find the Time?* inspires you and enables you to not only be more productive in the office and double efficiency but also achieve balance and discover the motivation that leads you to personal development, thus paving the path to professional growth.

Enjoy the journey!

Ready, Set, Go

I was working as "Acting CFO" of a psychiatric facility when a call from a recruiter came in that would change my life. One of the largest medical-surgical hospitals in the area was looking for a manager of accounting and reporting. The pay was slightly higher, but I wasn't sure if I wanted to give up a CFO title to work as a manager, even if "Acting" preceded it. However, reimbursement for psychiatric hospitals had been decreasing rapidly. I felt that our psychiatric hospital's days were numbered.

Every day, fixed departments were asked to assist the hospital flex staff based on the volume of patients. I remember having to register patients, accompany them to lunch when they required one-on-one care, and do _anything_ to help our struggling hospital survive. I did it willingly. It was exciting to know I was making a difference.

When I announced to the corporate office management that I was resigning, the Vice President of Human Resources flew from the corporate headquarters to the city where I lived to persuade me to stay.

He offered me a CFO position at a smaller facility. This role would allow me to train and eventually move to a larger hospital. However, I would have to work in another country and face a long commute.

After carefully considering my options, I decided to take the manager position at the medical-surgical hospital, which was one of the largest in the area. However, it was also facing financial difficulties.

Little did I know the challenges ahead.

The Challenge

Shortly after I started my new job at the medical-surgical hospital —which I will call ABC Hospital— I realized how much trouble it was in. Cash was going down fast, triggered by continued losses. Morale was low. In addition, the hospital was in the newspapers constantly, and not for good reasons. Almost every day, we were receiving calls from reporters.

I was a middle manager who didn't frequently deal with operations but was responsible for producing and explaining financial results, a task difficult to achieve in an environment with a deteriorating financial condition triggered by heavy losses. You hear these words frequently in such an environment:

"Don't kill the messenger."

Well, *I* was the messenger, and it was not easy to watch the *horrified* expression of my superiors each time I presented the numbers.

Something had to be done.

I needed to prove my value if I planned to survive the inevitable staffing restructuring already looming on the horizon.

The two largest costs at a hospital are *labor* and *supplies*. These had to be the focus of any cost-reduction strategy.

Executive management hired consultants to analyze the staffing and make recommendations. An internal team reviewed medical supplies to ensure competitive pricing and facilitate standardization. In addition, the efforts to change the hospital from a public enterprise to a private, not-for-profit entity began. This change would allow the hospital to move from the Florida State retirement system to a less expensive plan, which would result in millions of dollars in savings. Management had no option. The survival of the hospital and thousands of jobs were at stake.

The number of days-cash-on-hand had reached a dangerous thirty. **The hospital was thirty days away from closing its doors**, and employees had started to leave the organization.

Within six months of my arrival, approximately 80% of the accounting staff had left. Other departments were also affected by the financial situation, which resulted in Accounts Payable and Payroll being moved under my supervision. Within a couple of months, 50% of the Accounts Payable staff had resigned. Unemployment was very low then, and finding qualified applicants was difficult.

I needed to stop the bleeding and convince the best people of those who remained to stay.

I met with one of my senior accountants, who, for the purpose of this book, I will call Tom. Tom was a very capable employee who, in my opinion, had not been utilized to the fullest because of his "take-no-prisoners" demeanor.

It had taken me a while to gain his trust. Shortly after I hired him, he challenged me openly in two staff meetings. I had to act swiftly. I called him into my office and didn't waste any time.

"Do you have a problem with me?" I asked him, looking at him seriously, almost defiantly.

I had just turned thirty.

Fifteen years earlier, when I arrived in the United States, I didn't know English and was unfamiliar with my adoptive country's culture. I was married at eighteen, became a mother at nineteen, and approximately three years later, I started college, all while working full-time.

For several years, I had spent over fourteen hours most days working in the office, attending college in the evenings, and studying after my son went to bed or during my lunch breaks.

Sometimes, the stress of not understanding what I was reading, of having to translate every word, and the sleepless nights took a toll, making me question my fortitude. But my son's smile, the way my five-year-old kissed me on the cheek and walked me to bed—after I had fallen asleep over a textbook—gave me the determination I needed. I obtained a Bachelor's degree in accounting and graduated with honors.

The obstacles I faced all of those years helped me mature beyond my years, something Tom, who seemed a few years older than me, had not anticipated. In addition, having lived in Cuba as a child, growing up without my father, and lacking many of the most basic necessities in life had made me determined to take advantage of all the opportunities in my path. I owed it to my mother and to the country that had opened her arms to our family.

But going back to Tom.

My "Do you have a problem with me?" question seemed to take him by surprise. He then told me about his previous experiences within the organization, including his rise and fall from grace.

"Look," I said, "I can't do anything about what happened in the past, but I can tell you this. You're smart, and I like working with smart people. Let's work together to increase efficiency in the department. If we succeed, I will do everything I can to get you a promotion."

He agreed. We began to work on a plan right away, first by assessing the available technology and determining whether we were taking advantage of all the system's functionality. Then, we analyzed the job of each individual to identify inefficiencies inherent in accounting processes. Lastly, we took an inventory of all the reports we needed to produce on a monthly basis and began to build the tools to automate their preparation.

How Do You Find the Time?

This was before more robust systems became the norm, but the principles used then apply nevertheless.

My boss couldn't understand how, despite the attrition-related cuts, we could not only keep up but perform the work more accurately and in half the time.

Knowing how particular my boss was about the appearance of reports, I didn't want to say, at first, that we had automated the financial statements and contractual models using linked spreadsheets and databases, the only tools we had at our disposal, given our outdated accounting system and the lack of capital funds to replace it. After three months, she finally asked:

"How did you do it?"

I showed her what we had done. We improvised by making use of the existing technology to automate the creation of month-end reports and analytics. She was very pleased with the results.

Necessity is the mother of invention. Create that necessity. The urgency of a task drives you to action.

One of my favorite statements is:

Where there is a will, there is a way.

If managers create a "can-do" culture within their departments, the possibilities are endless.

How does a manager create an environment that leads employees to believe that <u>anything is possible</u>?

Here are some ideas, but you will find more throughout the book:

- Encourage and celebrate process improvement at staff meetings

- Conduct brainstorming sessions with your staff about the issues that hinder efficiency

- o It's surprising how many times I hear about managers who do not question their employees about the challenges they face. This is an essential ongoing communication.

- Provide employees examples of tasks that seemed impossible that were accomplished through innovation

- Challenge employees to innovate within their own areas

- Tell employees: "I believe you can find a way"

- Encourage employees to work with their team members on a solution

Eventually, true to my word, I managed to get Tom a promotion, which, after a few years, led him to more responsible positions. As I told him from the beginning:

"In an office environment, he or she who knows how to manipulate data to create meaningful and *timely* reports is king."

What makes you the king in the company where you work? Figure it out and master it!

To identify other time-saving ideas, I used a technique that had been around for years, one I strongly believe in: "Management by walking around." It's surprising how much one discovers during these walks.

But it wasn't just the walks; it was the questions I would ask the staff:

"Is everything okay? How can I help you make your work better?"

Many employees were truthful about the challenges they faced, which led to the identification of solutions and increased efficiency.

For example, I noticed all the busy work that was going on in Accounts Payable. Expanding electronic vendors was critical, but the effectiveness of electronic vendors depended heavily on updated pricing in purchasing, which would minimize the number of discrepancies. The more invoices that could be processed without human intervention, the higher the efficiency.

In addition, some departments were habitually late in approving invoices, causing Accounts Payable to make numerous calls to the department, not to mention the calls they received from unhappy vendors.

In a hospital setting, clinical managers are so busy caring for the patient that they often don't realize how these delays in invoice approvals can affect their operations, especially when vendors place the company on credit hold.

Accounts Payable's job was to educate these departments during face-to-face meetings and to show how timely approvals would benefit both areas. Frank and honest communication is key.

How Do You Find the Time?

The telephone is sometimes too passive of an approach.

At this point, those of you who are <u>not</u> managers might ask, *"How do <u>I</u> apply these concepts?"*

Think of your job. Think of those processes that take an extraordinary amount of time. If you step back and analyze them critically, you <u>will</u> find ways to make them more efficient, either through the use of technology or through modifications to the standard way of doing things. Ask yourself these questions:

- Could you decrease the frequency of some tasks?

- Could system-generated reports or uploads help avoid data entry?

- If you deal with customers, could you provide them access to the tools they need in order to reduce the number of calls?

- Could you receive training on programs that allow you to improve efficiency?

> *The key is to challenge yourself and others.*

Which is exactly what the leadership at the hospital did. They challenged middle management to work with less.

Not everyone liked the idea of working in such an environment. Those who were not up for the challenge left, leaving the hospital with the right people to make effective time management a reality.

Save Time, Save Money

As a young middle manager with experience working in environments where cash was in short supply, I had a few tools at my disposal, one being persistence.

In addition, four years before joining the medical-surgical hospital, I had worked as a manager at an air carrier company where cash was so low that I had to beg our business partners to fuel our single-engine airplanes.

The cash shortage had resulted from a new acquisition. The owner had purchased a highly leveraged company in another state without consulting anyone.

When I reviewed the books of the new company, I told the owner things no one should tell their bosses if they expect to keep their jobs. But he knew me well enough to realize I had good intentions. In addition, the cash flow analysis I showed him told him the entire story.

Our cash would be depleted in a year if we didn't obtain additional clients, a task difficult to accomplish in a very competitive environment. Many bigger players had the advantage of economies of scale and were crushing small companies like ours.

I had done everything I could to save the small business.

I learned the job of each of the consultants, for which the owner was paying a significant amount of money. I outsourced payroll to ADP, worked with our banks to provide funding, built a computer program to manage our aircraft maintenance needs, and then, of course, begged for fuel to keep our airplanes in the air.

In exactly one year, as I had predicted, cash had been virtually depleted. The business could no longer afford me, and sadly, I had to move on.

After that, I went to the psychiatric hospital, not as a patient, but as a temporary employee.

As soon as the CFO noticed my skills, I was promoted to manager, then to Acting CFO when my CFO left a couple of years later.

And many of you know what happened to psychiatric hospitals in the 1990s. Reimbursement simply dried up. It was a race to the bottom. As I mentioned at the beginning of the book, I found myself not only trying to manage the dwindling cash balances and working to improve efficiency but also helping other areas of the hospital keep operations going.

At the psychiatric hospital, I learned about many of the operational aspects of a hospital, from patient registration, insurance verification, billing, collections, and patient flow. I had to assist in those areas when the patient census unexpectedly increased, and the hospital could not afford to hire additional staff.

These experiences were excellent tools to have in my arsenal.

ABC Hospital was my third cash-stranded employer. Was it my destiny to work at struggling companies?

If it was, I was up for the challenge.

I began by learning and understanding every job in the accounting department. As I sat with each employee and asked them about their daily responsibilities, it became evident that by making small adjustments to various processes, we could save a significant amount of time. I also found that employees were performing substantial non-value work.

For example, accounting rules allow two different methods of amortization for premiums and discounts. One can utilize the simplest method if the impact of doing so is not material to the overall financial presentation. In our situation, it was not.

Yet, we were spending an extraordinary amount of time building worksheets based on the more complex method.

I continued to meet with staff, compile lists of tasks, and streamline the work. I will elaborate later in the Time Studies chapter on how this was accomplished.

These operational reviews should not be a one-time event. As the company continues to evolve, as staff leaves, these reviews must continue.

Although the example above relates to an accounting department, the concept applies in any setting. We will examine how at the end of this chapter.

Outcome:

After a few months, my department managed to complete double the amount of work it performed previously, with half the staff. Most of the staff cuts were accomplished through attrition. It was double the work because, by then, we had established a staffing company for which our accounting staff was responsible, plus our operations were increasing in complexity.

My workload in the office became greater than before, which meant that I also had to make adjustments in my personal life to save time.

My husband and I worked about a mile from each other then, which allowed us to carpool to work. Once we realized the benefits of carpooling, we have been doing it for the past thirty years. This saves not only gas and car expenses but also *time*.

We are stuck in traffic for up to two hours each day. I bring my computer or the reports I need to review and spend the entire time working, either writing my books or doing office work.

We have been carpooling for over fifteen years, and this and other time-saving techniques have allowed me to write three books.

Today, I'm writing this book as my husband drives us to work and listens to the news. The heavier the traffic, the longer it takes us to get to work, and the more time I have to write.

How Do You Find the Time?

Let's do this exercise:

- List everything you do during each work-day in a typical twenty-four-hour period
- Combine the hours for similar tasks
- Determine the percentage spent on each task
- Examine the list carefully

Let's assume that your list looks like this:

Task	Hours per day	Hours in 52 weeks*	%
Have breakfast and get ready for work	1	260	4%
Commute to and from work	2	520	8%
Time spent at work	10	2,600	42%
Cook dinner	1	260	4%
Watch television	3	780	13%
Sleep	7	1,820	29%
	24	6,240	100%

*based on five workdays (excludes weekends)

Ask yourself:

What can I control?

We all need to sleep, work, and eat, so that leaves us commuting and watching television. In this example, you are spending 13% of each workday watching television. Imagine if you were to reduce that time to one hour. You would save 520 hours (2 hours X 5 workdays x 52 weeks). This does not include the weekend. Imagine all you could do in 520 hours.

What about your commute? Can you carpool some days so you can free up time to do other things? Imagine how much you could do during your commute: pay bills, plan your week, and even write (which is what I did).

Have you ever measured how long it takes for the water in your shower to warm up? Most people just stand there and wait. This is precious time. What do I do? I make the bed.

Every minute counts.

Over the years, I have continued to identify new ways to save time in the office and at home. When peers, family members, and friends notice how much I can accomplish during a week, they often ask me:

"How do you find the time?"

How Do You Find the Time?

In the next chapter, we will examine the foundational elements of time management.

Time Management Essentials

In preparation for time management presentations, I've developed key tools to assist organizations in controlling this valuable asset. To successfully manage time, you must conduct a critical assessment of yourself and others around you. The next few chapters will be devoted to this conceptual preparatory framework. Think of it as the foundation of a house or the root system of a tree.

Time Management – Where to Start?

Understand and Manage Self	What are your stresses? What are your motivators? Understand what is the optimal level of anxiety Know your talents, skills, and knowledge Understand that change is inevitable

Understand and Manage Others	• What are others' stresses? • What are others' motivators? • Assess talents, skills, and knowledge of others • Coach and develop • Maintain realistic expectations

Understanding and Managing Self

The first step in creating the foundation for effective time management is to conduct a critical assessment of the self. Answering the following questions may assist in understanding what drives you. Writing the answers often leads to a more honest assessment:

- **What are your stresses?**

Remember that stress is not necessarily bad. A healthy level is essential to achieving professional and personal growth.

For instance, public speaking was a significant stressor for me.

What did I do to overcome it?

I forced myself to speak in public and even became a regular speaker at a university and for professional organizations.

The first time I stood in front of a crowd, I thought I was going to faint. My hands turned to ice, sweat gathered on my forehead, my legs trembled, and I felt dizzy. *You can do this,* I told myself.

I took a deep breath and announced:

"You have no idea how much I dislike speaking in public. I truly hate it, so I apologize in advance for the awful presentation I'm about to make."

A few people laughed. I focused and managed to get through it.

Admitting to my listeners that I was uncomfortable helped break the ice, possibly reduced my audience's expectations, and humanized me.

How Do You Find the Time?

I have learned several techniques to deal with stress. Here are some I have found to be very helpful:

- ❖ Take a deep breath and hold it for five seconds. Then, release it slowly

- ❖ Count backwards slowly

- ❖ Think of a happy place and mentally transport yourself there

- ❖ Smile

- ❖ Stretch gently

- ❖ Meditate

- ❖ Exercise

- ❖ Cry (not in front of people)

You may ask yourself how crying can be a stress reliever. When facing difficult situations, such as the loss of a loved one, the illness of a spouse, or highly stressful days at work, crying reduces stress. Avoid crying at work, especially in front of people, as some managers may view crying as a sign of weakness and inability to handle stress.

Multiple articles have been written about the subject of crying as a stress reliever. *The Health Benefits of Crying,* published by netdoctor.co.uk, suggests that tears could "actually be a way of flushing negative chemicals out of the body." A biochemist at the St. Paul-Ramsey Medical Centre in Minnesota found an "important chemical difference between emotional or stress-related tears and those simply caused by physical irritants, such as when cutting onions." Emotional tears "contained more of the protein-based hormones prolactin, adrenocorticotropic hormone, and leucine enkephalin (a natural painkiller), all of which are produced by our body when under stress."

o Why is having a good understanding of your stressors important in time management?

Imagine working for a boss who is a micromanager who is always looking over your shoulder. Does that management style stress you? Could you be as efficient working for a boss who functions at that level or with one that allows you a certain level of freedom?

If you understand what activities or situations stress you, you can more effectively utilize techniques to reduce that stress until performing those activities or handling those situations becomes as natural as breathing.

If receiving negative feedback affects your performance, don't dwell on it. Take a brisk walk, drink a glass of cold water, make corrections to the process, and move forward. Dwelling on situations that stress us isn't healthy or productive. This is once again where emotional intelligence comes into play.

- **What are your motivators?**

Are you motivated by financial incentives, a better work environment, work-life balance, and the ability to provide a solid future for your family? What drives you?

If you understand what motivates you, you will be better prepared to master time management. Motivation is a significant driver that can lead people to perform tasks they never thought possible.

Self-motivation ignites excitement and the determination to achieve results.

Self-motivation is to time management what oxygen is to a human being.

For example, as my mother approached the end of her life, she made me promise her that I would publish a book based on her life. I had been working on it for several years, but I wasn't happy with the product, and that discouraged me.

It wasn't until she died that I truly found my motivation to fulfill her final wish. That motivation fueled and focused my energies.

How Do You Find the Time?

Before I committed to publishing her book, I made an inventory of my skills. I had been writing since I was six years old, but I never had a formal class about character or plot development.

I joined a writers' group and even published a short story in a literary journal, but I felt this was not enough. I needed to learn more about the craft.

This analysis led me to develop those skills by attending a graduate certificate of creative writing program at the University of South Florida after I had finished my two Master's degrees in business and accounting.

I knew nothing about publishing, cover design, or marketing a book, so I had a steep mountain to climb to achieve success.

I worked at the office during the day. Then, I went home, cooked dinner, and began to write. I also reduced the time I spent watching television to about an hour a night.

How Do You Find the Time?

My husband loves to read, so I sat next to him and wrote while he read books about history and politics. I researched how to design the interior of a book, how to create a new company, and how to find the best editor. I also read about the experiences of other authors.

A critical decision was whether to go through the traditional publishing mechanism or self-publish through my company.

I have always been a control freak. I admit it. No use hiding it from my readers. I wanted that control. Therefore, I decided to publish my books through my own company.

Your motivation does not have to be as drastic as mine. Seeking the well-being of our families, especially our children, can provide significant motivation to push ourselves beyond our limits.

Remember, you will only grow when you are willing to step outside your comfort zone. Don't be afraid to do so!

- **Understand what is the optimal level of anxiety:**

An optimal level of anxiety is essential to achieve efficiency. On the other hand, being overly anxious all the time can lead to serious health issues. Each person has a different tolerance for stress, but without creating some level of urgency, we will not be as efficient as we could otherwise be.

The following question illustrates this point:

When are you likely to perform more efficiently, when you have a deadline, or when you don't?

In order to improve efficiency, whether at home or work and make the best use of your time, <u>utilize **self-imposed deadlines**</u>. Tell yourself: "I have to finish this by _____(fill in the blank)."

This technique will drive you towards the achievement of that task.

- **What are your talents, skills, and knowledge?**

    o **Talents**: Innate ability to do something. An example would be playing the piano by ear.

    When I was five years old, my mother paid for piano lessons for me, but I did not want to take the time to learn it. Instead, I preferred a more immediate satisfaction. I would always tell my professor: *"Either you play it first, or I won't play it!"* He always did. I would then sit down and replicate it without reading the sheet of music: *"You will never be a serious musician,"* he would say. But my goal wasn't to be a serious musician. I just enjoyed playing.

    Few people possess talents. If you are one of the fortunate few who do, recognizing it will lead you to manage time more efficiently when working on tasks that make use of your talents.

In the case of the musical piece, how long does it take for someone to learn a new song? It depends. It can be hours or days. But if he or she has the talent to be able to play by ear, the time required to master a piece can be substantially reduced.

o **Skills**: Learned ability to do something, including virtually any profession or skilled position.

You may be skilled in spreadsheets, databases, plumbing, accounting, and anything else you learn. Sometimes, when you master certain skills, they appear to be talents.

Who will be the most efficient accountant? One who knows advanced Excel and database functions, or one who has no clue about how to create pivot tables or v-lookups?

Generally, a skilled handyman can do a job faster than someone who does the same type of work infrequently.

○ **Knowledge**: Knowledge is the practical or theoretical understanding of various subjects. It relates to the familiarity with those subjects. It is different than skills in the sense that skills are developed through repetition or training.

For instance, my husband is very knowledgeable about politics and current events because he is always researching and reading multiple newspapers or listening to podcasts.

My years of experience in healthcare have allowed me to learn about various aspects of the business, including strategy, reimbursement, managed care, billing, and collections. I'm not necessarily skilled in these areas, but having general knowledge can make me efficient when dealing with specific issues that require my input, as I do not have to seek that knowledge from someone else.

<u>Understand that change is inevitable</u>:

Change will occur, and there is nothing you can do to stop it. Those who cannot adapt and evolve will fall off the train, so we must continue to renew and reinvent ourselves.

How is this important to time management?

Technology and people change and evolve, impacting the time it takes to complete certain tasks. This awareness of our environment is key in time management.

For example, banks have a feature that allows users to set up automatic payments and make deposits from cell phones. As a landlord, I am often surprised by people who are not familiar with the automatic payment feature. Once the automatic payments are set up, renters don't need to worry about writing a check each month, thus saving a significant amount of time.

Are all your utility bills automatically drafted from your account? What about car payments?

If you work in an office, learn the new features associated with software upgrades and how these features may impact your responsibilities and potentially save you time.

Software programs like Microsoft Excel and Access have far more advanced functionality than they did a few years ago. How can you capitalize on that functionality to become more efficient?

Emotional Intelligence:

You've heard this term over and over again. It refers to the ability to keep one's emotions in check.

It's easier said than done, especially if you, like me, are a hypertensive.

It's important to find a way to keep emotional outbursts out of the equation. I admire people who can do this consistently, but there are many ways to deal with our emotions: yoga and other forms of exercise, gardening, fishing, or writing. Each person is different, but finding an outlet and balance is critical.

Once your emotions are in check, you will find it easier to work in an ever-changing environment and deal with those who may not be emotionally intelligent. Why? Because you've been there. You've stepped in their shoes and know what it's like to be in their situation.

How does emotional intelligence affect time management?

Let's assume that your department has one employee who's constantly creating discord. You know that if you do not confront this individual, efficiency and morale will suffer. By having the emotional intelligence to discuss the situation and not letting his or her outbursts affect your self-control, you will be able to deal with the situation more swiftly. The conversation could take this form:

"Thank you for meeting with me this afternoon. We must discuss aspects of your behavior that are disruptive to the department, like the two times this week when you yelled at two different vendors on the telephone. This is not acceptable. We must treat each other with respect. I believe you have the talent and skills to be successful, and I would like to work with you on a plan that allows you to manage these reactions. Before we do, is there something that you would like to discuss that might be impacting your behavior at work?"

Whenever you find an employee who does not seem to have the emotional intelligence to succeed, don't write him or her off. Talk to the employee. Get to the bottom of the problem. You cannot always save someone from themselves, but at least try. Managers who are willing to work with employees who might be deficient in specific areas can not only save thousands of dollars for their employers but also improve morale and efficiency in the department.

Here are some elements of emotional intelligence:

1. The ability to anticipate changes or reactions. This includes being able to anticipate questions from customers in order to be prepared to respond to them.

2. Maintaining control.

3. Conceptualizing, planning, setting realistic goals, and adhering to plans.

4. The ability to work well independently or as part of a group.

5. The willingness to inspire others and self.

6. Leading by example.

When you have successfully mastered these elements of emotional intelligence and you understand yourself, you will have part of the foundation necessary to master time management. In the next chapter, we will examine how to understand and manage others.

Understanding and Managing Others

Whether you manage others or not, your ability to perform well within a team depends greatly on your ability to understand and work well with others.

- **What are others' stresses?**

Do you know what stresses your boss? Do you know what stresses your colleagues? Have you stopped to think about it? Why is it relevant to time management?

How Do You Find the Time?

Assume you manage a team that has multiple priorities. Your boss calls you:

"This has to get done!"

Your role is to support your boss, so you must spring into action.

You cannot say: "We have too much on our plate." That will surely *stress* him or her.

What do you do?

"How soon do you need this?" you ask. "I am currently working on _____(fill in the blank), but if this is needed right away, I can prioritize this task."

When confronted with multiple conflicting priorities, this communication is critical. Never assume your boss knows exactly what you are working on. Remember that her plate can be as full (or fuller) as yours, not to mention the added stresses associated with higher-level positions.

How Do You Find the Time?

If you never ask that question or explain what tasks you're working on, your boss will assume that you can handle the new assignment. If you and your team worked fifteen hours in one day to get it done, you may have effectively changed her expectations for future projects.

If you continue to subject your staff to an excessive number of hours, morale will suffer. Also, the longer someone works during the day, the lower the efficiency.

I cannot emphasize enough the importance of effective communication in time management.

When I analyzed the individuals who have reported to me throughout my career, I noticed some who did very well during stressful times but others who became nervous and frustrated. Knowing this has allowed me, during critical times, to tap into those individuals who handled stress well.

A manager needs both types of employees. Perhaps those who crumble under pressure can do the day-to-day tasks, while those who shine and outperform when exposed to stress can handle ad hoc, time-critical projects.

Understanding who can perform in what settings will result in improved efficiency and happier employees.

This is not to imply that employees should be categorized and kept in those categories. When times aren't as busy, employees should be provided with the tools to help them acquire additional knowledge, gain confidence, and grow.

- **What are others' motivators?**

What motivates your employees? What motivates your customers and peers?

Motivated employees are likely to be more efficient than those who are not. It's not always easy to motivate employees. For example, how do you motivate people who work in transactional areas, such as Accounts Payable and Payroll?

How Do You Find the Time?

Those teams need to know that you care about the problems they're facing. Teambuilding activities that give them a sense of belonging goes a long way in creating a workforce that's motivated and willing to go the extra mile.

In addition, what about a suggestion box? Our department has one placed by a tall wooden cat that wears a badge (the wooden cat belongs to one of our directors). Silly, I know, but employees love it.

I provide staff with financial incentives whenever they suggest money-saving or time-saving ideas. In fact, **employees are encouraged to lead the implementation of their ideas.** If you show employees that you trust them enough to assign leadership of those tasks, their trust level will increase, which will lead to improved efficiency.

If you don't manage employees, how do you determine what motivates others? And why would you care? How would knowing that save you time?

How Do You Find the Time?

Let's examine this scenario:

One of the employees in the department has earned frequent awards due to her productivity. You would like to know what she's doing so you, too, can perform at her level and become more efficient. You've asked her, but she has not been willing to share any ideas with you. What can you do?

Knowing what motivates this employee is critical. Is it recognition? If so, you might say: "I'm very impressed with your skills. What do you suggest I do to improve my speed?"

If she likes doughnuts, you might bring some one day. Build a relationship with that employee. Fostering a good relationship with peers can lead to the sharing of ideas that result in improved efficiency.

Assess the talents, skills, and knowledge of others:

Managers must be acutely aware of the expertise of their employees. This will allow them to divide the work in a manner that will produce optimal outcomes in the minimum amount of time.

However, assessment is only a part of the process.

Coach and develop:

Although it would be wonderful if we could hire employees who possess all the skills necessary, that's not realistic. An employee may have a stellar resume and perform well during interviews, but after the hire date, the areas for improvement begin to emerge. It can happen. This is also part of setting realistic expectations, which we will cover below.

Coaching and developing employees is an important part of managing time. Coaching can produce extraordinary results. Managers must be willing to fill the knowledge gaps they notice in their employees.

Tips for coaching employees:

- Don't be afraid to discuss how employees can improve
- Show them examples of areas to improve
- Don't be judgmental, but be honest
- Be a facilitator

Through the years, I have seen many examples of employees I hired either out of college or even high school and, through coaching, blossomed into professionals.

I remember a young woman who was a single mom at a very young age. I could see the fire within her, but she lacked focus. I was tough, yet I gave her multiple opportunities, even on one occasion when I caught her with a small television set under her desk. She was only eighteen.

I spoke often with her through the years and encouraged her to pursue an education. She became a stellar employee. Eventually, she received a Bachelor's degree in accounting.

How Do You Find the Time?

Unfortunately, I didn't have a position for her when she finished her degree, but she became a successful accountant at a local firm. One day, she visited me and said:

"Thank you for everything you did for me. For the first time in my life, my mother told me that she was proud of me."

That's one of many stories.

It's a struggle for some of my high-performing employees to leave because they enjoy the environment, but my goal is to give them wings and let them fly. In the process, I've had committed and dedicated employees who have produced results.

Over the past eighteen years of my career, my department has not had any audit adjustments, something difficult to achieve in a 1 billion dollar operation.

Coach and develop. Your investment in your employees will undoubtedly improve efficiency.

Maintain Realistic Expectations:

Be realistic about what you can expect from your employees and those around you. Don't expect perfection because you'll be disappointed. Realize that despite people's best efforts, they will make mistakes. It's part of being a human being.

Create an environment that minimizes the opportunity for errors but realizes they will occur from time to time.

In certain environments, like healthcare, where lives are at stake, there's no room for error, and efficiency takes a backseat to quality. In these environments, the key is that leadership needs to provide the resources required to produce consistent quality outcomes. Once the quality is consistently achieved, leadership can focus on reducing the length of stay.

Stages of Time Management

Through my years managing people and learning about organizational behavior, I have developed a conceptual framework to assist leaders in managing time effectively.

You will notice that goal-setting is at the core of time management.

Why goal setting?

Having a goal allows you to visualize the end game. If you focus _all_ your energy on the satisfaction that comes with attaining your goals, that alone will drive you towards achievement. That "oomph" is contagious, making you and others achieve things that were never thought possible.

Goal-setting is like the heart or glue that holds all the components of time management together.

How do you set goals?

Goals must be:

> Specific
> Attainable
> Answer the questions:
  o What
  o When (over what period of time)
  o How much?
  o Who?

Here are some examples:

❖ I will write twenty pages per week over the next ten weeks
❖ I will run ten miles a week over the next twelve weeks
❖ I will complete a creative writing class within six months

❖ We will increase revenues by 10% over the next twelve months

Goals can also be long-term, like the typical bucket list.

Many years ago, my husband gave me a book about 500 places one should visit. I did not believe we would even make it to the first 50, but we set a goal of visiting at least five of those places per year. Some years, we visited as many as ten cities, which allowed us to check almost one hundred cities off the list so far. We accomplished this by booking multi-country cruises and reducing the amount we spent on restaurants and clothing.

Goals drive us to action.

Let's do an exercise:

- Write down three realistic goals on a large piece of sticky paper

- Place your list on the refrigerator door

- Read your goals every day

- Examine what happens to your drive to achieve those goals

Stages of Time Management

Scheduling:

Scheduling is the process of organizing your available time or other valuable resources in order to optimize workflow. As schedules are set, it is important not to take on more than can be handled during a specific period. Doing so leads to inefficiency.

In setting up an effective schedule at the office:

How Do You Find the Time?

- Consider travel time to and from meetings

- Build contingencies for unexpected events (this may include a backup)

- Make a realistic schedule that takes into account the complexity of the meeting and the agenda

- When deliverables are expected as a result of a meeting, write a list of tasks or prepare a more formal project plan

Manufacturing firms, hospitals, and physician practices depend heavily on effective schedules. In addition, management's schedules at organizations ordinarily include a number of meetings. Between meetings, managers spend their time organizing tasks, problem-solving, and creating project plans. To ensure the most efficient use of the available time, a project plan or a list of tasks should be maintained and periodically updated.

Lists of tasks are critical to organizing work not only at the office but also at home.

Let's examine the following scenarios:

How Do You Find the Time?

Sarah gets up at five that Saturday morning. She cannot possibly sleep for one more minute, as there is too much on her plate, so much so that she hopes that she is able to remember it all. First, she had to pay the water and electric bills. She tells herself that she should have taken the time to set up the "auto-pay" transaction with her bank, but who has time for that?

As she is about to go into her account, she tells herself: "Let me see what's new on Facebook." She closes the bank program and logs on. By seven, she's still reading stories on Facebook. Then she remembers. *My sister is coming to our house this afternoon, and my house is a mess.* Forget the bills. Now she has to clean the house.

Her husband wakes up. "Honey, can we watch the last episode of *Dr. Who* that I recorded?"

She looks at him and thinks about it. The house has to get cleaned, and bills have to be paid, but he wants to watch *Doctor Who*!

She doesn't want to fight. He *is* the love of her life. Oh well, one hour won't hurt anything, but once that episode ends, he wants to watch another. At eleven, she takes a shower and gets ready to go out to lunch at their favorite Chinese restaurant, a routine she and her husband had established when their son left the house when he was eighteen.

She accomplished nothing.

Consider a modified scenario:

Sarah is up at five that Saturday. She knows her husband gets up around seven, so she writes down the following list:

1. Pay two bills
2. Clean the house
3. Wash and dry clothes
4. Organize business papers
5. Write a short inquiry to the home-owners association about a misapplied payment
6. Watch television with my husband
7. Lunch

She consults the clock again. She has to focus and prioritize, which means that placing the dirty clothes in the washer should be the first task, as it takes forty-five minutes for a load to finish washing and another forty minutes in the dryer. As the clothes wash, she logs into her bank account and not only pays the bills but also sets up automatic payments.

She thinks about her Facebook friends, yet when she consults the list, she realizes she does not have time for that. She checks each item as she finishes it and moves on to the next, watching the clock to make sure she has enough time to accomplish it all.

By the time her husband is up at seven, her first five items have been checked off, and this makes her feel energized.

"Do you want me to cook you some breakfast?" She asks her husband.

His eyes open wide, like a child who just won a prize, and he happily nods and embraces her. Sarah smiles and cooks him his favorite scrambled eggs recipe.

They sit down in front of the television set and eat their breakfast while watching *Doctor Who*, and after they're done, he places the program on hold and offers to wash the dishes. In the meantime, she goes to the bedroom to make the bed and organize things.

In conclusion:

Lists and the ability to remain focused on the task at hand can more than double efficiency.

Cell phones generally have an application for notes. Most people carry their cell phones everywhere they go. Why not write your personal list on your phone for easy reference?

Effective Delegation:

Some managers are reluctant to delegate because they're afraid tasks won't be completed in accordance with their expectations.

However, managers must create the right conditions for effective delegation to occur. They must first focus on organizing the work, and here, it is important to emphasize the importance of lists again.

Be sure to:

- Create checklists of tasks that need accomplishing, as well as who is responsible for those tasks
- Ensure employees work from their individual checklists
- Check off tasks as they are completed
- Select samples of the employees' work to review or verify (sampling depends on the type of activity)

What about at home? How does one effectively delegate at home?

Going back to the previous example, what if Sarah had ten tasks on her list? The only way she could get through all of those tasks would be to delegate some to her husband.

How Do You Find the Time?

When it comes to family, there is a positive and a negative way to ask a loved one for help.

Positive:

"Sweetie, would you mind helping me with these tasks?" said Sarah.

"But I wanted to watch *Doctor Who* episodes!" said her husband.

"I'm so sorry, but we're going to incur late fees if we don't get this done. It shouldn't take very long," she says with a smile as she kisses his cheek.

Negative:

"Can we watch Doctor Who?" asked Tom.

"Watch Doctor Who? Do you know how much is on *my* plate? When am I supposed to get through all this? Do I look like a robot to you?" Sarah said.

I've been married for over thirty years, and sometimes, work is very much like a marriage. Do you think that the couple that utilizes the second approach will last? Do you think that any relationship would endure that type of discourse?

Don't sacrifice relationships at the expense of time management. You can have both a wonderful relationship and effective time management, but you must respect others.

Treat others the way you would like to be treated.

When I started to work at ABC Hospital, I did not know how to delegate effectively. I was afraid that all tasks would not get done. An important step in achieving effective delegation is to hire people you can trust to do the right thing.

To be able to trust others, you must create the right environment. You must show employees that you are worthy of their trust. It's a bidirectional exchange.

Trust and Review:

Trust not only fuels the economic engine worldwide, but it also drives everything we do. Customers do not purchase goods from companies they don't trust. Similarly, CEOs are most likely to hire someone with a high level of integrity. Organizations must create an environment of trust in order to improve efficiency. Creating such an environment involves:

- Hiring trustworthy employees

- Fostering cooperation and mutual respect

- Communicating effectively when situations arise to threaten trust

- Soliciting input from employees to resolve issues

Entrusting employees with a task does not mean that managers walk away. The process of review and verification is essential, no matter what type of business you're in.

Managers get busy between meetings, e-mails, problem-solving, and new initiatives, but it is important to set aside time for review and verification. In some environments, verification is more critical than in others, but unfortunately, managers cannot always verify everything their employees do. There is simply not enough time.

What do they do?

Let's assume that Sarah manages an accounting department. Her staff is responsible for over two hundred reconciliations. How can she possibly review all of them?

Here's one approach:

➤ Prioritize and stratify

➤ Sort the accounts by materiality (high to low)

➤ Review all the highly material reconciliations and a selection of the medium and low-materiality accounts

➤ Select a different group from medium and low materiality groups during the review

➤ Realize that although Sarah trusts her staff with her life, she is ultimately responsible for the work they do

How does *trust and review* work at home?

How Do You Find the Time?

Let's illustrate:

Sarah and Tom are married. They both deposit their paychecks into one bank account. Sarah and Tom prepared a budget together, but she ensured adherence to that budget. At the same time, Tom is responsible for general maintenance at the house: changing the air filter from the air conditioning unit, taking out the garbage, feeding the birds, and fixing anything that breaks.

Each one of them is entrusted by the other to perform their tasks, but what about verification? Can this occur effectively?

The verification process in a marriage occurs more naturally. Sarah and Tom both take turns opening the mail so Tom can easily confirm that the bills are getting paid. They agreed that the filter would be changed on the first day of every month. Therefore, she may casually ask him:

"Sweetie, did you change the filter?"

This division of labor saves time and money and creates a harmonious relationship. However, be careful. The last thing anyone needs in a marriage is the appearance of mistrust.

Managing Expectations:

Having unrealistic expectations can be detrimental to time management. Likewise, customers should be educated on when to expect specific deliverables. Advances in technology are making this easier to accomplish. For example, when a credit card or service payment is made through the bank, once the vendor and amount are entered, a message appears telling the user when their payee can expect payment. This eliminates the need for multiple calls or emails to the bank.

Educating your superiors, customers, and subordinates plays an integral part in the management of expectations.

Let's illustrate this concept with another example:

Sally is an analyst for the budget office. She supports multiple managers and directors. At any given time, she may be working on a number of projects that she will need to prioritize. None of her customers know what is on Sally's plate, which may lead to multiple status e-mails and calls. These unnecessary non-value-added activities reduce the time Sally has to take care of her customers' needs.

If Sally initially spends some time educating her customers on what to expect, she will have happier customers and will be able to spend more time on value-added activities.

➢ **Can Sally say no?** The answer is it depends on the situation. Sometimes, saying no to her boss can be a career-ending move, but she could educate him or her about what's on her list. She might be inclined to say no to a friend or family member. Yet, in order to preserve a good relationship, she should communicate why she's unable to help. When it comes to peers, she has options.

Let's review this example:

Sally is responsible for report writing and is the company's subject matter expert. Following a major implementation, the requests from multiple users keep coming, but she is just one person, and no matter how much work she has taken home, there are only so many hours in the day.

One approach is to meet with her requestors to decide as a group what reports should have priority. Another is to ask her customers to prioritize their requests. She should then distribute the list to all of her customers with the timeframe for completion. This reduces calls and frustration.

Sally should also discuss the number of requests with her manager, as sometimes it is not possible to wait, in which case additional resources might be required.

Disruption Management:

Disruptions are unavoidable. They are an integral part of any workplace, but there are ways to minimize them.

1. If you have an office, you might decide to close the door and place a sign on it, such

as: *Working on a critical project.* Many people will understand this and avoid disturbing you, but others may consider you unapproachable and rude.

2. If you work in a cubicle, you might consider placing a sign at the entrance of your cubicle. Be creative. You can draw a happy face above it if you like. After all, you must preserve a good working relationship with your peers. But does that always work? Some people a couple of cubicles down from you may consider you rude.

3. What about moving to an empty office or conference room or asking your boss to allow you to work from home? Consider your environment, determine what is or what isn't acceptable, and act accordingly.

4. Accounts Payable departments may consider having their customers call within specific times or communicate with the appropriate clerk via email.

5. Provide your customers with the appropriate contact for urgent matters.

6. Educate your customers about your processes (this cannot be emphasized enough).

Can disruptions occur at home?

Of course. Constantly. The telephone rings, vendors or neighbors knock on the door, your aunt Thelma visits you unexpectedly, or your significant other wants you to read the latest tweet from the president. You cannot completely avoid disruptions at home, but you can minimize their impact. For example:

1. Tell your family members to call within a specific timeframe.

2. Depending on the situation, you might decide to let the telephone go to voicemail.

3. If you need to pay bills, write, or do anything else that requires concentration, find a quiet room in your house and close the door.

Prioritization and Automation:

Prioritization is the logical arrangement of tasks, high to low, based on criticality. When prioritizing tasks, it is important to consider automation.

Below is a list of questions that you should answer:

1. **Is there a way to automate the most time-consuming processes?**

   Let's assume that your staff is preparing bank reconciliations. Is there an interface from the bank to the accounting program showing checks that were paid? If a company has to process thousands of checks each month, who has the time to determine which ones have been cashed manually?

   Think about your home life. Are your utility bills automatically drafted from your account? If you pay rent or mortgage, are you using the automatic payment feature that is available with most banks?

As I mentioned earlier, I have spoken to many people who do not know that this feature is readily available. As of the writing of this book, it doesn't cost anything. Imagine your bank writing the check on your behalf every month and mailing your payment. You don't even have to pay for postage. Not only does this save you time, but it saves you money.

2. **Is the appropriate person completing the task at hand? In other words, does the individual possess the appropriate skills?**

This example illustrates this concept:

When Alice started to work at a psychiatric hospital, it was supposed to be a temporary job. There was nothing else available, and she was tired of sitting at home.

Her role was to assist the hospital in bringing general ledger reconciliations up-to-date in preparation for an audit. The CFO di-

vided the work between her staff accountant and Alice.

After a few days, her boss noticed that Alice had finished a significant number of
reconciliations compared to the staff accountant, and she provided much better
support. In addition, Alice identified thousands of dollars in unclaimed property re-
coveries.

What did Alice's boss do? She offered Alice the position of Assistant Controller and
eliminated the staff accountant. In order to
justify her title, she also moved Accounts
Payable and the business office functions
under Alice's supervision.

Some of these concepts apply at home as
well (except the opportunity for promotion
or pay increases).

If you have a significant other, are you di-
viding the housework to tap on each of
your skills? If your significant other is better with computers and math, it may take

him or her less time to reconcile a bank account.

Who is more organized in the kitchen, you or your significant other? Organized people typically spend less time preparing the same meal.

3. **Are you periodically reevaluating processes to make sure that you have automated the tasks that can be automated?**

Even if you have automated the most time-consuming tasks, continued reevaluation must be part of your normal routine. Why? Because most businesses are always changing. In addition, technological changes provide us with more efficient avenues to perform tasks.

4. **Have you removed duplication?**

Often, multiple departments utilize or report the same data. This not only results in inefficiency, but if each department presents different data, credibility suffers. Here is an example:

William generates a monthly income statement for the company where he works as a senior analyst, and he is responsible for explaining the results of operations. Every month, a significant amount of money is spent on pharmaceuticals. Therefore, each month, he downloads the purchases and analyzes them. Did the price of high-cost drugs increase? Is the company purchasing a higher volume of expensive medications?

He wasn't aware that an analyst within the pharmacy was conducting the same analysis. However, when he was discussing the results of the month with the pharmacy director, he casually mentioned it. The pharmacy could save a significant amount of time by relying on William's work. Instead of having to compile the data, they could devote their time to explaining it.

Collaboration improves efficiency and productivity within the organization, as well as the timeliness of deliverables.

Time Studies

What is a time study?

Various definitions exist, and this one takes the most common to another level. A time study is a systematic approach designed to determine how much time and effort is needed to complete specific tasks. It is also a process to identify those tasks that take the longest to complete and the processes that must be implemented to improve efficiency.

There are many ways to conduct a time study. Some companies utilize consultants. Others utilize an internal engineering department to survey employees. We have discussed some of the elements in previous chapters, but let's dig a little deeper.

First Step:

1. Ask each employee to provide a list of their responsibilities and how long it takes to complete each task.

2. Ask each employee to identify the most time-consuming duties separately. Some companies prefer not to rely on employees to provide this information. Instead, they might ask an analyst to sit with the employee and time each task. For more standardized activity, companies may rely on benchmarks.

   At this point, it is important to note that even though many managers think they know what their employees do, many do not. Turnover changes the dynamics of a department, or conditions change.

Second Step:

How Do You Find the Time?

1. Meet with those employees who share similar duties in a conference room and discuss each of the most time-consuming tasks.

2. Determine, as a group, how to improve efficiency.

3. Include someone from IT or within the department who possesses strong technical expertise in the meeting.

Surprise! Meetings like this one accomplish many goals:

1. Employees will feel, and rightly so, like a key part of the process.

2. You will give your employees a voice, and by doing so, you will uncover qualities in them you may have overlooked before.

3. You will identify redundancies in the processes.

4. You will reduce the time it takes to complete each task by brainstorming ideas.

    a. As an example, when I met with hypothetical employee Tom, I noticed that every day, he was uploading information from the bank into the accounting system. I asked him if there was a reason to do this every day. The answer was no. Then why do this so often?

b. Understanding the underlying reasons why employees do a specific task, and the frequency at which they do it is a critical step in defining potential solutions.

5. The meeting should result in a solid plan that employees will embrace, as *they* were and are part of the solution.

If you don't manage others but find that it is taking too long to perform certain tasks, realize that people like to help, and they like to be asked. Here is what you can do.

➢ List your most time-consuming tasks

➢ Identify someone you trust who possesses strong technical skills

➢ Ask him or her how they would automate some of these tasks or do things differently

How Do You Find the Time?

➢ *Remember, sometimes, you're just too close to the information to be objective*

Your manager will be impressed that you took the initiative to improve a process.

The Power of Positive Thinking

What does positive thinking have to do with time management?

Look around you, at the people you know at work or personally. Who is likely to be more efficient? If you're questioning yourself constantly, your own thoughts will hinder performance.

Try the following for the next three days:

- Get up every morning, look at yourself in the mirror, and say: "Today is going to be a great day!"

- When you arrive at your place of employment, smile and say good morning (or good afternoon) to your peers. No matter what happens, think positive thoughts, such as:

  o I *can* do this

  o This is easy

  o If someone who I do not consider as smart as I am can do it, why can't I?

  o I am smart

  o I am capable

  o I can make a positive change in my life

  o Life is good

What do you think will happen to your performance and efficiency?

Positive affirmations impact behavior.

According to The Johns Hopkins Medicine article, *The Power of Positive Thinking,* "researchers suspect that more positive people may be better protected against the inflammatory damage of stress. Another possibility is that hope and positivity help people make better health and life decisions and focus more on long-term goals. Studies also find that negative emotions can weaken immune response."

This article also discusses the benefits of smiling. "A University of Kansas study found that smiling—even fake smiling—reduces heart rate and blood pressure during stressful situations."

Surround yourself with positive thinkers. Be a catalyst for positive change.

As I was growing up, my mother used to tell me often: "Smile, and the world will smile with you."

On the day that we went to make the arrangements at the funeral home after my mother's death, my sister began to make jokes about my mother's casket and about the things that my mother would tell my father when she arrived in Heaven. Most people would have been devastated and full of grief, but my sister chose to laugh instead. After a while, as we sat by a round table, we both laughed so hard about silly things that even the person assisting us was almost in tears. Moments later, I reminded my sister that we were at a funeral home. As she tried to remain serious, she started laughing again.

Her laughter made me get through one of the most difficult moments of my life.

Positive thinking can sometimes heal. I questioned this until I witnessed it. Someone in my husband's family had been diagnosed with cancer and given a few months to live, but she never let the diagnosis sadden her. She continued to cook for her family every day while her daughters worked. She used to tell people: "If my day comes, so be it, but I will go on with my life until God decides."

She never let her diagnosis define her. She went through chemotherapy, and one day, the doctors told her that her cancer was gone. Her family believed it was a miracle. What do you believe?

Part II

How Personal Development Can Lead to Professional Growth

Growing as a Human Being

No matter where employees are in the organizational structure, they all deal with many of the same issues. They might feel insecure, unappreciated, and doubtful. Realizing this, managers must learn to seriously consider the people skills necessary so that they can provide employees with the confidence and trust they need to be successful.

Many studies reveal that happy employees can lead to increased productivity. *The Harvard Business Review* has published multiple articles on happiness at work and productivity. One of these articles suggests that happy employees can increase productivity by as much as 31%, with three times the amount of creativity.

A May 2016 *Quartz* article concludes that "the key to happiness at work" is not money but autonomy. Employees who can set their own goals and can make at least some of the decisions on their own are happier.

There are certain measures managers can take to empower employees:

1. Let each employee run a staff meeting.

2. Ask employees to submit educational ideas. For example, my staff meetings typically include an employee education agenda topic. I have taught them healthcare metrics, such as the meaning of FTEs, length of stay, case mix, and other language unique to the healthcare setting.

   What information would your employees like to learn about their place of employment?

3. Ask your employees what you could do to make their jobs easier. This can be very useful. Here is an example:

When the Payroll department at ABC Hospital went under my supervision, I noticed that a significant number of employees suffered from carpel tunnel. I immediately requested workstation evaluations for each of them. A nurse who specialized in these matters reviewed posture, equipment needs, and chair quality. Often, I would have to spend $500 to $700 per employee to bring workstations up to acceptable standards.

Conclusion: New carpel tunnel incidents were eliminated. Employees became happier and engaged, and efficiency improved. In addition, costs decreased, as the hospital no longer had to pay thousands of dollars to injured employees.

The following ideas can improve happiness in the workplace without increasing costs significantly:

1. A monthly birthday cake.

2. Adding employees' birthdays to the manager's calendar and having the manager send a personal note during birthdays.

3. Acknowledging employees with a "good morning" or "good afternoon."

4. When family issues emerge, provide them with flexibility within reasonable parameters.

5. Try not to deny vacations. This is a standard practice I've followed for years in professional environments.

   Here is an example of how to accomplish it:

   a. During a new employee orientation, explain the following:

   "I don't deny vacations. However, it's up to you to ensure adequate coverage during your absences. Work with your peers. Involve me if necessary."

6. Requiring overtime should be avoided. Instead, ask employees if anyone has the flexibility to work extra hours. In those rare cases, when you don't have enough volunteers, what about a different approach? Consider meeting with your team and have them determine who can work extra time as a group.

7. Celebrate team play.

8. Encourage team activities.

    a. If you work at a large organization, consider having someone speak to your employees about stress management or similar topics to improve their lives at work and home.

9. Don't wait until evaluation season to inform employees that they need improvement. Identify the concerns well in advance and work on a plan with them.

10. Be honest. Honesty goes a long way. If you find a deceptive employee or one that exhibits behaviors that aren't appropriate,

face the issue immediately. Delays will negatively impact performance. Here's an example:

a. Sarah noticed that an employee was often away from his desk. One day, when she asked him where he had been for the last two hours, he said he was at a coworker's office going over an outstanding problem. Sarah decided to verify what the employee told her and determined that the employee had not been truthful. What should she do? Is this grounds for termination?

Sarah should meet with the employee immediately. She needs to understand what's causing the employee to be away from his desk for an extended period. She could say:

"I learned that you were not truthful with me. If we're to continue working together, we need to function in an environment of trust. Credibility is difficult to achieve, but it can be lost very rapidly. I will give you the opportunity to earn my trust. If you're open and honest with me, I'll do the same with you."

This approach works. Don't write off employees too quickly. It's expensive to replace them. During my career, I've seen many successful turn-around stories. It's worth it to try. The result could be a thankful employee who will go out of his or her way to help you achieve your goals.

11. Be careful when enforcing tardy policies: Life happens. Employees can be late for a number of reasons. In all my years of management experience, I can only think of two occasions when I found myself in a position to have to enforce a tardy policy after giving an employee a number of opportunities to rectify the situation.

12. When handling employee issues, ask your-self: "How would I like to be treated?" Treat employees with the courtesy you expect from your superiors, and the result will be happy employees, which will lead to efficiency in the workplace.

Work-life balance is also important. The 2017 Harvard Review article *If You Want to Be Happy at Work, Have a Life Outside of It* illustrates this point. However, as this article indicates, people sometimes "have a poor understanding of what makes them happy."

Exercise: What makes you happy? In order to help you make this assessment:

- Write down on a piece of paper the things for which you are thankful
- Read the list out loud
- How does that make you feel?

This exercise should make you focus on the positive aspects of your life.

Personal Development: How Did I Find the Time?

The impact of personal development cannot be understated. I can recall a statement from one of the leaders who interviewed me for a position:

"I voted for you to get the job because I was impressed with the fact that you played the piano. In terms of job skills, you were in line with other applicants."

Her vote helped me get hired.

Likewise, professional and personal networks can help you land the right job or obtain additional skills. However, in addition to gains associated with those networks or skills you have acquired, lifetime learning is essential to professional development.

If you love to write, dance, play an instrument, or play sports, take the time to develop and perfect those skills.

If you're afraid of public speaking, take a class.

You never know how the networks you develop or the ongoing learning might help you achieve professional growth.

Here is how writing *Waiting on Zapote Street* helped me.

As I mentioned, my mother passed away in 2011. Since our arrival in the United States, she would tell everyone:

"One day, my daughter will write our story."

She never saw her dream fulfilled, but during her last few years of life, as she fought cancer, she made me promise I would publish her story. We met as often as we could to document it, afraid her time would run out. She, too, began to write in journals, which she would eventually leave me upon her death.

I worked full-time and helped in her care, which made it difficult to devote a significant amount of time to writing, but I also didn't have the incentive or the maturity to finish her story.

It's amazing how much one changes after the death of a parent, especially a mother.

Her death impacted me greatly on an emotional level, which made it difficult for me to read her journals without breaking down. When I finally built up the courage to do it, what I discovered was an intangible treasure.

It became an obsession to fulfill her final wish. I wrote during every waking hour, after and before work. It was therapeutic to write. In a way, it was almost like bringing her back to life in the pages of my book.

Little did I know how much the publication of this book would transform my life?

How Do You Find the Time?

In 2015, *Waiting on Zapote Street* began to open its doors.

A board member I knew, who had read the story, connected me to the president of a major local magazine, who then connected me to a group of professional women seeking to expand female participation on boards of directors. At this meeting, I met an assistant to the governor of the State of Florida. As soon as she heard my story, she told me: "The governor would love to talk to you."

She suggested I apply for an open position at the Hillsborough Community College Board of Trustees.

When this opportunity presented itself, I was thrilled. My mother was a teacher in Cuba and had been a tutor in the United States. For years, she had instilled in me and others the importance of a college education, and here I was, about to start where she had left off.

How Do You Find the Time?

My participation on this board allowed me to help bring millions of dollars into my community and to advocate at the state and federal levels. It has helped me understand the critical role of board members in organizations in-depth and has expanded my professional network.

In 2016, a United Nations book club selected *Waiting on Zapote Street* for reading. The excellent review it received helped me market it to other individuals. Eventually, more book clubs picked it up.

In 2017, *Waiting on Zapote Street* made the list of top ten books on The Latino Authors' website. It also became a #1 bestseller on Amazon.

My network continued to expand. One person would tell another. I received many letters and comments from all over the United States and even from readers abroad as my book began to expand its international presence. Update: By 2024, I had already published sixteen books!

In addition, I was asked to speak to professional organizations about the book and time management.

Following the success of *Waiting on Zapote Street*, I published *Candela's Secrets and Other Havana Stories, The Dance of the Rose, Havana: A Son's Journey Home, and twelve other books.*

How did I manage to do it all?

I've discussed some key ideas throughout the book, but in addition to practicing these concepts:

1. I've set various goals throughout my life. Here are some of them:

Goal: By the time my son reaches the sixth grade, I want to send him to a private school.

Shortly after our son was born, my husband, our newborn, and I moved to a single-wide trailer. My husband and I were nineteen years old then. I worked at a Winn Dixie, and he worked at a furniture warehouse. Many times, we hardly had enough money to pay for food. It was under those conditions that I set this goal. People thought I had lost my mind when I told them, but I persevered.

This goal led me to work all day and attend college in the evenings. It also drove me towards graduate education and energized me to excel at work and the university.

Try this:

Write down a goal and tell people about it. Don't give up. Keep working towards it until you achieve it.

Goal: I want to pay off my house by a specific date.

After living in the trailer for five years, my husband and I purchased a tiny house that was smaller than what we could afford. We also continued to drive used cars.

After selling our first home at a profit and buying a second one, we lived there for a few years. We also sold the second home at a profit and bought a third one. We committed to paying off our third house by a specific date and managed to achieve that goal.

How?

Not only did we invest the profits from the first two homes into our third house, but when other friends were going to restaurants, we were eating at home. We had a few vacations then. We car-pooled to work, bought only the clothes we needed, and watched every penny. We continued to save money as if we were still making mort-gage payments. By the time the real estate market collapsed around 2010 and 2011, my husband and I began to invest in real estate.

Goal: I want to finish my mother's book by my fiftieth birthday.

This goal drove me to finish her story and pub-lish it a couple of weeks after my birthday.

Goal: I want to make my mother proud for as long as I live, even if she is no longer here.

How Do You Find the Time?

This long-term goal gave me the drive to become involved in the community and continue to market her book. I reinvested the proceeds from this first novel in the publication of other books, like this one, that might help other people in their journey through life. I've also donated some of the proceeds to charity.

2. I focused on and dedicated myself fully to every goal.

3. I gave myself realistic deadlines.

4. When a door closed, I convinced myself that another door would open.

5. I found many angels during my journey, people who were unselfishly willing to help me. I could not have done it without them.

6. I helped others less fortunate along the way.

   A friend told me once that I was blessed because I was always helping someone.

   "I do not expect anything in return," I told her.

"That is why you're blessed," she said.

7. I kept telling myself: where there is a will, there is a way.

8. I planned and had high expectations of myself and others.

9. I practiced other time-saving ideas:

   a. I cooked the food for the week on weekends and froze it.

   b. I purchased healthier frozen dinners when I consumed them with homework on the weekends.

   c. Slept fewer hours. I realized that I could function well with five to six hours of sleep. Not everyone can do this, but after five o'clock, I often found myself looking at the ceiling, even on weekends. Why not do something with that time?

   d. Set aside time to write every weekend.

e. Set aside time to write during our vacations.

f. Utilized the time spent taking showers for planning or plot development. I was surprised by how many scenes I developed when taking a shower. After I finished, I would run to the computer and write down the ideas until I could go back to them.

g. Resolved complex issues in the middle of the night.

Does that happen to you?

I heard other people say that this happens to them as well. Assume you had a busy day at work. A complex problem surfaced, and you could not think of a solution. Then, in the middle of the night, you wake up and identify the solution. It never fails to amaze me when that happens.

h. After setting up a major goal, I set up small, incremental goals. Some people need small wins to keep going. Give yourself those small wins.

My major goal now, in addition to bringing my mother's story to people around the world, is to help others do things they never thought possible. One of my readers, who always wished she could teach one day but didn't think she could find the time to do it, applied at a local university and obtained a part-time job as an instructor. I saw her a year later. She was thrilled to be teaching while still working full-time.

Even some of my co-workers have found the inspiration they needed to take them to the next level.

When we as individuals do something that some might consider extraordinary, then extraordinary things can happen to others who are inspired by our actions.

Inspiration can drive not only individuals but also organizations. Employees who feel inspired can use their intrinsic motivation to help an organization achieve extraordinary change.

As a manager, never underestimate the impact that motivation can have on employees. Help them reach new heights.

Life is What You Make of Your Time

I'm finishing this book on the day of my son's thirty-third birthday as we sit in the lobby of a hotel in White Plains, New York. Both my husband and my son are reading on their devices after we spent a nice day enjoying the surrounding towns.

I could be watching television, but I chose to do something more productive with my time.

How Do You Find the Time?

Life is about what we choose to do with the little time we have on earth.

Within one family, we often see those who succeed professionally and those who don't. We see individuals without a college education, whose natural talents allow them to become inventors and earn six-figure incomes, and those with college degrees who go nowhere. The opposite can also be true.

What differentiates people who succeed from those who don't?

Clearly, some individuals' success is tied to their parents' ability to pay for tutors and a good college education, but what about those who were born into poor families?

For example, Oprah Winfrey's mother was a maid. Oprah ran away from home at age thirteen after being sexually abused and becoming pregnant. Her son was born ill and died, and eventually, Oprah went to live with her father.

How Do You Find the Time?

From early on, she knew she wanted to focus on a career involving speaking or drama. Her talents in these areas allowed her to become student president while attending Nashville East High School.

During her senior year, she entered a public speaking contest. She was awarded the grand prize: a scholarship to Tennessee State University, where she majored in speech communication and performing arts. However, due to a job offer, she was unable to finish college. Yet, her confidence in her speaking ability led her to send her tapes to the right individual one day. Not much later, her show was born. Over the years, she has continued to conquer new heights.

According to the *Sydney Morning Herald*, she sleeps five-and-a-half hours each day. This undoubtedly has been attributed to her success, but additionally, she has incredible drive and stamina. Her focus is a big part of her achievements. She can go for months without watching television.

How Do You Find the Time?

If you stopped watching television and using social media, how many hours would you save each day?

We have discussed a number of concepts in this book aimed at saving time and improving efficiency, from goal setting, utilizing lists, and prioritization to disruption management. We have also explored how personal development can lead to professional growth.

As you identify ways to enhance your quality of life through time management and personal growth, do not forget about life itself.

I'll step outside the coldness of a business book for a moment to share a statement that appears in *The Dance of the Rose,* a novel based on my family's life.

To give you some background, Laura, one of the main protagonists, is sitting by a window watching a couple work in her yard as she reflects on the past. She has lived a full life and is thankful for her family and the years she lived on borrowed time, but she realizes the end is near:

"Life is temporary glimpses of happiness. It is about loving with intensity and leaving a mark on the world. Its fleeting nature is not to be feared, but to be embraced with every fiber of our being, with the knowledge that tomorrow does not belong to us, yet we may shape it with simple gestures of kindness."

My mother said a variation of this statement during the last few days of her life. If there's one thing that I'm grateful for, other than being a mother to my son, it's having a wonderful husband and having the best brother and sister one can have. I'm glad I found the *time* to care for my mother during the years she fought cancer and when she took her last breath.

As we make choices during our professional careers, it's important that when we get to the end of our lives, we have no regrets.

How Do You Find the Time?

Mastering time management is as much about careful planning and removing non-value-added activities from our day as it is about finding a balance.

I often find it interesting how, after working a ten-hour day, I can attend a community college award ceremony and be re-energized. When I hear the story of students and what they do to succeed, it feels as if my inner battery is replaced with a fresh one.

How can you find an outlet that allows you to refresh your inner battery and, at the same time, achieve the impossible?

Time management is about finding what drives us and others. It is about searching for the motivation to leave our mark on the world and make it a better place through our actions.

Acknowledgments

I would like to thank, with all my heart, the people without whose contributions and commitment this book would not have been possible:

My mother, my source of inspiration for everything I do. I was a teacher, a mother, a father, and a kind person who, above all, believed in the promise of America.

Maria Fernandez (my aunt), for being such a cheerleader and telling so many people about my books, even her doctors and the people at the supermarket. Thank you and my uncle for raising me and for instilling in me the idea that anything is possible.

Lissette (my sister) and Jeff Riley, for all the support during my journey as an author. Lissette, thank you for accompanying me during book signings and for being the light of my books.

Cecilia Martin, for helping me promote my books and encouraging me during the writing process.

Ivan Viamontes (my husband), for helping me with edits and for supporting me for over thirty years.

Madeline Viamontes (my mother-in-law), for listening to my stories and cooking for my husband and me every Saturday to allow me to focus on my books.

My readers, for reading my books and writing your comments on Amazon. An author would be nothing without someone who reads what she or he writes. Thank you for all the love and support.

Raquel Henry, a wonderful editor, writer, and friend, and the owner of Writer's Atelier. Raquel is a caring and giving individual who supports writers in her community.

References

- https://en.oxforddictionaries.com/definition/time

- http://www.imdb.com/name/nm0001856/bio

- *Oprah's sleep habits: seven-minute wake-up window and five hours a night.* The Sydney Morning Herald. October 13, 2015

- *The Health Benefits of Crying.* www.netdoctor.co.uk

- Achor, Shawn. *The Happiness Dividend.* Harvard Business Review. June 23, 2011

- Zilca, Ran. *If You Want to Be Happy at Work, Have a Life Outside of It.* Harvard Business Review. March 9, 2017

- Cooper, Belle Beth. *The Key to Happiness at Work Isn't Money, It's Autonomy.* Quartz. May 4, 2016

About the Author

Betty Viamontes was born in Havana, Cuba. In 1980, at age fifteen, at the height of a massive Cuban exodus from the Port of Mariel in Havana, she immigrated to the United States with her mother and siblings.

Mrs. Viamontes completed graduate studies at the University of South Florida and moved on to a successful career in Accounting. She also completed a Graduate Certificate in Creating Writing.

She has over twenty-five years of progressive management experience at healthcare organizations. In addition, she has published *Waiting on Zapote Street*, an autobiographical novel that continues to expand its international reach, *Candela's Secrets and Other Havana Stories,* an anthology of short stories and poems, *The Dance of the Rose,* a mother-daughter memoir-style story, and various short stories and poems that have appeared in newspapers and literary magazines.

Betty Viamontes is passionate about education. She is a regular speaker at the University of South Florida and other professional organizations and currently serves on the board of Hillsborough Community College. She also served as Chair and Vice Chair of the FICPA Healthcare Conference Committee in 2017 and 2016, respectively.

She lives in Florida with her husband and family.